Wonders of the Cactus World

SIGMUND A. LAVINE

Illustrated with photographs

DODD, MEAD & COMPANY
New York

Illustrations courtesy of:
Biological Section: Department of Lands, Queensland, Australia, page 36; Carter's
Cactus Greenhouse, Tewksbury, Massachusetts, page 12, 15, 28 (left), 30 (bottom),
45, 48, 61, 65, 66, 67, 73 (bottom); Henrietta's Nursery, Fresno, California, page 8,
11, 14, 17, 20, 22, 24 (right), 26, 28 (right), 42, 54, 68 (top); The Metropolitan
Museum of Art, Gift of Nathan Cummings, 1964, page 44; National Park Service,
page 29, 41, 75; National Tourist Council of Mexico, page 56; Jane O'Regan, page 10,
16, 30 (top), 33, 64, 68 (bottom), 73 (top); Jane O'Regan (after Kramer), page 71;
Organ Pipe Cactus National Monument, National Park Service, page 39; Park Seed
Company, page 72; Saguaro National Monument, National Park Service, page 2, 51,
74; and U. S. Department of Agriculture, page 18, 34, 47.

FRONTISPIECE: *Close-up of the spines and ribs of* Cereus giganteus—
the saguaro

For Fred—
    Who supplies much of the paint that
    keeps my thumb green

Contents

ABOVE: Echinocactus grusonii, *the golden barrel cactus, has sharp yellow spines. Tuberculed when young, it develops ribs and a crown of yellow wool with age.* BELOW LEFT: *Even when not in bloom, the spines and the hairy areoles of* Mammillaria zeilmanniana *make it a desirable plant.* RIGHT: *Glochids (tufts) cover the edges of the pads of* Opuntia acicularis, *making it attractive even when not in bloom.*

1. "Many kynsfolke and few friends..."

Linnaeus, the Swedish botanist who originated taxonomy (the science of grouping animals and plants according to their natural relationships), created the word "cactus." He derived it from *kaktos*, the name given by the ancient Greeks to a prickly plant. While the identity of that plant has never been definitely established, it is assumed that it was a thistle.

It was appropriate for Linnaeus to transform *kaktos* into cactus. The majority of the plants to which he applied his new word are covered with tufts of horny spines which, in some species, are very sharp and powerful. Moreover, a great number of cacti are armored with barbed bristles called glochids.

Whether they are smooth or prickly, all cacti are classified as Cactaceae by taxonomists. They comprise a family of perennial herbs and shrubs furnished with areoles. No other plants have these unique organs of growth. While areoles have the appearance of tiny cushions, close examination reveals that they are actually small pits. From them spring branches, flowers, glochids, spines, and, when present, leaves. If the areoles—which are located on the stem—are removed, a cactus dies. Even the destruction of a few causes severe damage to a plant because the fuzzy centers of areoles act as insulation—they repel heat and retain moisture. The number of areoles on a particular cactus and their placement, along with the profusion and posi-

9

Cereus cacti have leaves only when seedlings. This young plant's leaves will soon drop.

tion of the spines, are used by botanists to identify its species.

As a general rule, the Cactaceae are plants with woody skeletons and extremely fleshy stems, and they usually lack leaves. However, certain cacti bear more or less full-formed leaves. Most of these plants live in tropical or subtropical jungles where rain is plentiful. Other cacti have leaves but drop them when their stems are fully developed. Leaves appear on still other species but they either wither quickly or are reduced to mere scales.

All the ancestors of modern cacti that lived along seashores some fifty million years ago when the Earth's climate was humid had foliage. Then, as their environment became drier, cacti adapted to the change by not producing leaves. How this has helped them survive in desert regions is fully discussed later in this book.

STEM

Very few individuals can identify every plant displayed at a flower show. But almost everyone can recognize a cactus. No other plants have such fantastically formed stems, which may be angular, columnar, fluted, globular, jointed, notched, ovoid,

10

ABOVE LEFT: *Like all hedge-hog cacti,* Echinocereus knippelianus *has beautiful flowers. It is easily raised in a small pot in full sunshine.*

ABOVE RIGHT: *The powder puff cactus,* Mammillaria bocasana, *is covered with fluffy hair.*

RIGHT: *Tephrocacti are low-growing opuntias whose stubby, globular stems are joined together in links. They are related to the prickly pears.*

ABOVE: Opuntia microdasys, *popularly called bunny ears, has flat, spineless pads covered with golden tufts of soft glochids. The plant on the right is normal, that on the left, a freak, or* monstrosus *variety.*

RIGHT: *Bristles topping* Melocactus intortus *resemble a fez— the source of its common name, Turk's cap.*

more or less ribbed, spiral, wavy, or winged. In some species the stem stands erect, in others it is prostrate or semi-prostrate. While many columnar cacti have a single stem, a number of species have stems that branch either at the base—where they very often form large clumps—or high above the ground. Frequently, when the upper section of a non-branching cactus is injured or dies, the lower part of the stem develops branches.

While the majority of cactus stems are grotesque, none are more outlandish in appearance that those that are fasciated— flattened out at the top and abnormally widened into rock-like masses, coils, fans, "hands," or crests. These extraordinary deformities are caused by irregular cell growth. Cells may be compared to the bricks with which a mason builds a wall. Just as each brick is a unit of the wall, cells, joined together, comprise all living things.

Fasciation malforms individual plants in practically every known species of cacti. But the chances of encountering cactus monstrosities in the field are slim. Only one plant in approximately fifty thousand of a species is fasciated. Nevertheless, cacti with deformed stems are sold by plant specialists. Some of these are cuttings propagated from fasciated specimens, but most are artificially created. This is done by making a shallow cut across the top of the stem with a very sharp knife—a process which may or may not achieve the desired result and frequently causes the plant to die.

Cactus stems may be as smooth as a rubber band or as prickly as a porcupine's back. Those in the latter group are covered with tubercules (wartlike growths) that are actually the stalks of the reduced leaves. Tubercules are overlaid with keen bristles. Many a careless windowsill gardener has become aware of the sharpness of these bristles while handling one of the mammillarias, perhaps the most popular of the Cactaceae. Indeed, anyone who has ever been "stabbed" by a mammillaria will agree that it is well named the "pincushion cactus."

SHAPE

There is almost as wide a variation in the shape of cacti as there is in the construction of their stems. The hugh columnar bodies of some species resemble exotic trees. Other cacti look like balls of various sizes. Still others are barrel shaped. Many of the small, fat, rounded types have the appearance of bizarrely designed buttons.

There is nothing fanciful about the form of vinelike cacti,

Two pincushion cacti. ABOVE LEFT: Mammillaria bombycina *has white "wool" and pink flowers.* RIGHT: *Flowers arise from hairy areoles at top of* Mammillaria magnifica.

BELOW LEFT: *Members of the genus Notocactus, ball cacti, are fine plants for amateur growers. They are small with brilliant spines, and flower freely.*

RIGHT: *It will be years before this* Ferocactus glaucescens *matures into a specimen barrel. Its clusters of yellow spines contrast with the light green body dotted with prominent tubercules.*

A cane cactus is easily mistaken for a leafless shrub.

whether they are prostrate or climbers. But the mimicry cacti—
as the name implies—are oddly shaped. One of the most interesting of this group is the *monstrosus* variety of the totem pole
cactus (*Lophocereus schottii*). This knobby-stemmed, spineless native of the American Southwest and of northwestern
Mexico looks like a column of lumpy green jade.

No mimicry cacti are as curiously shaped as those that look
like stones. All of these are very small plants, lack spines, and
are composed of more or less triangular or pyramidal tubercules which are either brownish or dark gray. Because of their size,
contour, and coloring, these low-growing cacti resemble bits of
stone. In fact, the popular name for *Ariocarpus fissuratus*, one
of the commonest of mimicry cacti, is "living rock."

As might be expected, the various "living rocks" are favorites
with those who raise cacti as a hobby. Most species are easily
obtained from cactus suppliers, while a few can be found
among the inexpensive plants sold in the flower departments of
supermarkets and department stores. However, some years ago,
"living rocks" were rarities. In 1840, a specimen of *Ariocarpus
kotschubeyanus*—a species that is easily mistaken for one of

the rocks that usually surround it—sold for two hundred dollars.

Besides varying greatly in form, cacti also differ greatly in size. The rebutia of South America—aptly nicknamed the Tom Thumb cactus—has a diameter of less than an inch. On the other hand, the Mexican ball cactus (*Echinocactus ingens*) may be nearly a yard in diameter, attain a height of eight feet, and weigh nearly a ton.

But the ball cactus is a pygmy to *Cereus giganteus*, the saguaro (sah-wah-ro). Called the "trademark of Arizona," this tallest of the Cactaceae may grow forty to fifty feet tall, be nearly three feet in diameter, and weigh some twenty thousand pounds.

It takes between 150 to 200 years for a saguaro to attain its full growth. A four- to five-inch saguaro is at least ten years old, a three-foot specimen approximately thirty years old.

Saguaros are not the only slow-growing cacti. Many other species take decades to mature. However, a number of these plants are highly prized by cactus collectors because of their

Most cacti grow very slowly. It will take about twenty years in the average household for the seedling on the right to reach the size of the mature plant shown.

LEFT: Oreocereus celsianus, *the old man of the Andes*
RIGHT: Opuntia vestata, *an old man from Bolivia*

appearance. One of the favorites is *Cephalecereus senilis*, which reaches a height of thirty feet in its native Mexico, although its annual growth rate is a little over two inches a year. Even a quick glance at one of these plants will explain both its popularity and why it is called the "old man cactus." Not only does the stem become gray with age but also it is covered with a matted beard of soft, whitish bristles that resemble hair.

Some cacti grow rapidly. None of these develop into fully matured plants capable of reseeding themselves more quickly than certain of the Opuntias. Because their edible fruits are protected by sharp spines, these cacti are called "prickly pears."

Habitat

Despite his cleverness in coining the word "cactus," Linnaeus' knowledge of the Cactaceae was very scanty. This was because he worked in the eighteenth century, long before most species of cacti had been discovered, studied, and classified. Moreover, the only specimens of the Cactaceae that Linnaeus and his fellow Old World scientists had the opportunity to examine were

Cacti growing on rocky mountain slopes

the few plants sent to them by friendly explorers or travelers. No cacti are native to Europe. In fact, with the exception of a small—and rather uncomfortable—handful of species found in parts of Africa, Ceylon, Madagascar and neighboring islands, cacti were unknown outside the Americas until Columbus carried some back to Spain.

There are nearly two thousand identified species of cacti. The majority of species are indigenous to the New World, and cacti can be found there in many places. Their range extends from Chile northward to Canada. Cacti grow in low-lying valleys or rain-soaked tropical forests, and on sun-drenched plains, rocky mountain slopes, and deserts. While the greatest number are residents of the tropics and subtropics, the temperate zone houses several species. The latter withstand the cold of winter because the snow that covers them acts as a warm blanket of insulation.

However, the greatest number of cacti are native to the arid regions of the southwestern United States, central South America, and Mexico. More different varieties of cacti grow in Mexico than anywhere else. In fact, nearly half of the classified genera (groups of related species) are found there.

While many different types of cacti abound in the New World, the Cactaceae of Africa and Asia show little variation. All of these plants belong to the genus *Rhipsalis*. Botanists debate as to whether or not these cacti evoluted in their present habitats or were originally planted by seed-carrying migratory birds, gale winds, or ocean currents. Since *Rhipsalis cassytha*—known as the "mistletoe cactus" because of the shape and color of its fruit—grows in both the Old World and the Americas, the scientific argument is a heated one. But whichever theory is correct, *cassytha* and certain of its allies are the only exceptions to the rule that the Cactaceae are exclusively plants of the Western Hemisphere.

Incidentally, the mistletoe cactus, like its namesake, lives in trees. So do a number of its relatives. But this is the only resemblance between the plants. Mistletoe is a parasite, sapping life from trees in the same fashion as fleas feed on dogs. Tree-dwelling cacti are epiphytes—plants that grow on other plants but do not take nourishment from them.

CLASSIFICATION OF CACTI

Scientists have divided the Cactaceae into three subfamilies. The first of these, the Pereskioideae, has very few members. But small as their numbers are, these residents of tropical America are of special interest to botanists—like their ancient ancestors some of the Pereskioideae bear large, fully formed leaves.

Of all the Pereskioideae, the genus *Pereskia* and its close relatives have the most fascinating habits of growth. All of them are thorny shrubs with woody, rounded stems. A number of these

LEFT: Pereskia gatesii. *Note the flat evergreen leaves which, unlike those of other genera, do not drop when the plant matures.* RIGHT: Hylocereus guatemalensis *has the jointed stems of the genus* Opuntia.

cacti climb. *Pereskia aculeata,* commonly called the Barbados gooseberry, is a ten- to twenty-foot-long vinelike cactus that clambers upward by means of the thorns in the leaf axis (the upper angle formed by a leaf with the stem). *Aculeata* is widely cultivated as an ornamental vine in the West Indies where it is known as the "lemon vine" because of the scent of its creamy blossoms.

The second subfamily, the Opuntioideae, is made up of the genus *Opuntia* and its kin. These cacti have fleshy stems and joints instead of leaves. However, seedlings of *Opuntia* have two cylindrical real leaves an inch or less long which soon drop.

Hairs, thorns, and bristly glochids with hooked tips cover the areoles of many Opuntioideae. This makes them extremely difficult to handle and, as a result, few are found in cactus collections. Among the exceptions to this general rule are the epiphyllums and certain opuntias.

The epiphyllums well deserve the popular name "orchid

cactus." The large tubular flowers come in all shades of red, varying hues of cream, greenish-yellow, lemon, pink, or are multicolored. A number are night-bloomers. The most spectacular of these is *Hylocereus undatus* ("Honolulu queen") which has two distinctions. Festivals are held in its honor in the Hawaiian Islands and many of the loveliest hybrid epiphyllums have been developed by crossing *undatus* with other species.

There are two types of opuntias. Those with flat joints are called "tuna" while species with rounded or cylindrical joints are known as "cholla" (choy-a). Some opuntias are treelike, others prostrate, climbing, candelabra-like, or bushy. Many are so prickly that they can only be handled with thick leather gloves or tongs. On the other hand, certain species are spineless. Besides varying in shape, size, type of growth, and armor, opuntias differ in their climatic preferences. As a result, opuntias of one type or another can be found from the tip of South American northward to Cape Cod in Massachusetts.

The great majority of cacti belong to the third subfamily, the Cereoideae. While even the non-expert can recognize the Pereskioideae by their leaves and the Opuntioideae by their joints, the Cereoideae have no "family resemblance." Some are towering columnar giants, others globular or low-growing plants without elongated stems, small clustering globes, or tiny cylinders. However, all of them bear spines. These may be straight, hooked, stiff, feathery, twisted, or erect. In some species the spines are camouflaged by a veil of silky hair.

No cacti are more popular with windowsill gardeners than the Cereoideae, particularly species of the genus *Mammillaria* (so-called because of its prominent tubercles). Not only do their hairs make them attractive but also the intricate patterns and coloration of their spines delight cactus collectors. These individuals also prize the mammillarias because of the small, bell-like flowers which crown the tops of the plants.

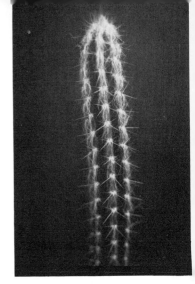

LEFT TO RIGHT: Mammillaria parkinsonii, *owl eyes, and* Mammillaria plumosa, *feather cactus, are favorites of windowsill gardeners.* Cephalocereus royensii *blooms at night.*

Actually, the mammillarias are very easy to bring into bloom. Nevertheless, it is a rewarding experience. Those who accomplish it for the first time are inclined to boast of their achievement almost as much as amateurs who successfully raise a "night-blooming cereus"—the popular name for several nocturnal species of Cereoideae.

NATURAL WATER TANKS

Cacti are among the most specialized of plants. Over the centuries they have developed structural features that enable them to survive in areas of much sun and little rain. The most important adaption they have made is the ability to store water in their thick pulpy stems.

However, water storage is not a unique characteristic of the Cactaceae. Hundreds of species of plants with sap-filled stems have the same capacity. They are called succulents—a word derived from the Latin *succus* (juice, sap).

Despite the fact that all cacti are succulents, botanists separate the Cactaceae from other water-storing plants. The experts

22

refer to "cacti and other succulents." This is not because of technical differences but for convenience. Cacti belong to a single family but the rest of the succulents are scattered among some twenty plant families.

Besides being succulents, cacti are xerophytes. Literally translated, this Greek word means "dry plants"—vegetation whose bodies are modified not only to retain water but to prevent its escape. As a result, xerophytes are ideally designed for desert life.

A number of taxonomists are not content with merely separating cacti from other succulents. They maintain that the Cactaceae have been placed in the wrong order—a category of plants having similar structure—because cacti blossoms have little in common with those of other vegetation. Therefore it is argued that the Cactaceae should be placed in an order of their own. But those who would make this change cannot agree on what the new order should be called. Some experts claim it should be the Opuntiales, others the Cactales.

While the experts dispute, cacti continue to thrive as they have for centuries in arid areas. When it does rain, their extensive tissue soaks up water like a sponge while the hard, waxlike coating of their bodies cuts down the loss of the precious liquid through their stems. Even in times of drought, water makes up 70 per cent of a cactus' weight. When its tissue is filled, 90 per cent of the plant's weight is water.

Just as bridge-builders leave small spaces between steel girders to allow for the seasonal expansion and contraction of steel, nature places ridges or protuberances on the stems of a cactus. These provide the necessary "give" when the tissue swells during wet weather. Conversely, many cacti become quite shriveled when unwatered for long periods. But once watered, the tissue becomes plump and firm within a few days. Thirsty cacti are greedy drinkers. Some of them absorb so much water that their

LEFT: *Denied water, this plant shriveled. But the stems became firm and plump once it was watered again.* RIGHT: *The ribs of cacti partially shade the body of the plant and thus help to conserve water.*

tissue splits, forming deep, long scars on the stems and branches.

The ribs which are characteristic of a great many cacti are also a water-conserving adaption. Actually fused areoles, they cast a small amount of shade on the body of the plant and thus partially shield it from the sun. Ribs are also a factor in photosynthesis, the process by which all green plants obtain the materials they need for growth. This consists of forming carbohydrates—compounds containing large amounts of sugar and starch—from carbon dioxide in the air and water. The larger a plant, the more carbon dioxide it assimilates. Since ribs enlarge the total surface of a cactus, they increase its capacity to photosynthesize.

The kitchen in which most plants prepare their food is their foliage. Leaves trap sunlight and use its energy to transform minerals from the soil (absorbed by plants in a dilute solution) and carbon dioxide into sugars and starches. The carbon di-

24

oxide enters the leaves through minute, mouthlike openings called stomata. At the same time, water evaporates from these holes. Scientists refer to this evaporation as transpiration.

Leaves pass a tremendous amount of water into the air. For instance, a birch tree with 200,000 leaves releases 700 to 900 gallons of water vapor daily. When rainfall is normal this loss of water is harmless but in times of drought the tree may die. Nevertheless, stomata must be kept open all through the growing season regardless of the weather in order to provide entrance for carbon dioxide.

Because most cacti are leafless, the Cactaceae transpire very small amounts of water vapor. Moreover, their stems—which are the centers of photosynthesis—are furnished with very few stomata. These, in turn, are either recessed or covered with hair, an arrangement that protects them from moving air. Transpiration is speeded up by air currents just as the rate of the evaporation in wet garments hung on a line to dry is increased by a wind.

Cacti also conserve water by keeping their stomata closed most of the day. While this limits their intake of carbon dioxide, they suffer no damage because they store the gas and draw on it when making food. Like most desert plants, cacti absorb carbon dioxide during the early morning and late evening. During these hours there is light enough to trigger photosynthesis, but temperatures are low. As a result, the stomata release relatively little water vapor. A giant saguaro expels less than a quart of water a day, but a date palm passes about five hundred quarts into the air every twenty-four hours.

However, in reducing transpiration and otherwise adapting to conditions unfavorable to most other vegetation, the Cactaceae have slowed down their metabolism. This is the chemical process which is constantly taking place in living things and which effects the building up and destruction of vital substances. Since their metabolic activity is sluggish, cacti grow slowly.

Roots

The well diggers of yesteryear always assured their customers, "We'll find water if we dig deep enough." They were right. Even in the driest of deserts, water lies beneath the sand. To reach the water, which may be many feet below the surface, some plants are deep rooted. But cactus roots, which are covered with a cork-like bark, do not penetrate deeply into the soil in search of water. They grow horizontally in the topmost three or four inches, spreading in all directions. This enables the roots to sop up moisture even in the lightest of rains. On the other hand, surface roots do not provide a plant with strong support and cacti are frequently blown over by strong winds.

Actually, it is only the older section of a root that holds a plant upright and pipes water to the stem. Moisture is taken in only by the growing ends of roots. Hundreds of tiny root hairs —each an extension of the root tip—surround the end of the root. These never become roots, their only function being to pull water from the ground.

While cactus roots may not be firm anchors, they are most efficient in supplying water and diluted minerals to the plant stems. The slightest dampness in the soil will stimulate the

Strombocactus macrochele is not beautiful but an interesting species. Note the thick root stock. The flat, flexible spines feel like paper.

growth of a veil-like mass of hairs on the root of a saguaro. When the tissue cannot absorb any more water, the root hairs die and the root itself becomes dormant. But when rain falls again—perhaps a year later—the root immediately becomes active.

All cacti do not have the same type of root. Some species have thick and conical roots that resemble the taproot of a beet. Other cacti are tuberous—their roots are stout and fleshy. A number of epiphytic species have aerial roots. But most of the Cactaceae have a relatively short, tapering root from which lateral rootlets branch. It is not an easy task to dig up a cactus that has fibrous (branching) roots without damaging some of these "water pipes." A cactus only three feet in height may have roots that extend ten feet from the stem in all directions.

SPINES

It would be extremely difficult to convince an amateur gardener who has handled cacti that the Cactaceae lack spines. But, technically, this is true. Spines are strong and sharply pointed bodies arising from the wood of a stem and represent branches or outgrowths. The needle-like projections of cacti are not connected to the tissue. Therefore, botanists classify them as thorns. However, scientific terminology is ignored even by professional cactus growers and the term "spines" is generally employed to describe the armament of Cactaceae.

Cacti are furnished with both true and false spines. The former—which may be as flexible as paper or as stiff as a spike—vary from an inch to over a foot in length. There is also a difference in the shape of the spines of various species. Some are straight, others are arched, cylindrical, flat, prismlike, or twisted. The tips of true spines also display diversity, being barbed, hooked, needlepointed, or almost blunt.

Because of their coloration, true spines give many cacti a

LEFT: *The fantastic patterns of their spines make cacti attractive house plants even when not blooming. Such specimens are best handled with leather gloves or a "collar" made of several strips of folded newspaper.* RIGHT: Astrophytum asterias *is a spineless species known as the sea urchin cactus.*

rather attractive appearance. While certain cacti have glassy or transparent spines, those of most species are shaded in various hues of black, brown, purple, red, yellow, or white.

But ornamentation is not the function of true spines, which serve to prevent grazing animals from feeding on cacti and also help spread the plants. An entire cactus or section of one frequently becomes pinned to an animal hide. When it falls or is rubbed off, it roots in a new location. Moreover, true spines help keep cacti cool by providing partial shade. They form a "Venetian blind" as their shadows move constantly across the stem while the sun passes from east to west. Finally, spines shield the stem from hail and protect it from plant-eating rodents and many injurious insects.

All true spines develop from buds. The Cactaceae have superimposed, paired buds. The lower one produces spines; the upper, flowers or branches. However, nonexperts can easily mistake the flexible, stiff, woolly hairs or long stiff bristles

28

The organ pipe cactus in bloom

The Easter cactus in blossom. Like the Christmas cactus, this plant is known as a crab cactus—each link of its flat, narrow stem has the outline of a clawed crab.

Few flowers are more beautiful than the vividly hued, bell-shaped blossoms of cacti.

found near the upper bud of many species for true spines. Certain of the Opuntioideae are also furnished with false spines. These structures resemble "a single row of long hairs knitted together." Similarly, certain spineless cacti are equipped with tufts of stout, sharp bristles that have the appearance of true spines.

FLOWERS

The exquisite beauty of cactus blossoms amaze those who see them for the first time. The wheel- or funnel-shaped blossoms are brilliantly colored brown, crimson, orange, pink, red, violet-red, white, or yellow and have a radiant metallic sheen. Moreover, the outer series of floral leaves (sepals and petals) which make up the floral envelope are most attractively formed. They may be acute, feathery, frilled, obtuse, rounded, or toothed.

Not only are cactus flowers magnificent in color and graceful in shape but also their structure is most unusual. They are composed of a great number of small segments and, unlike most other flowers, show no distinction between the sepals and the petals. Both of these grow from an upside-down tube of varying lengths and forms. All cactus blossoms have a great many pollen-bearing organs (stamens). In some species the stamens are so sensitive that if an insect merely brushes them, they close upon the pistil which contains the ovary where future seeds develop.

Cactus flowers are short lived. Those of certain species may last for a week or more but, in general, the blooms fade within two or three days. Many of the Cactaceae keep their blossoms open during the day and close them at night. Some species expand their flowers only when bathed in sunlight and keep them shut on overcast days.

On the other hand, certain of the Cactaceae are nocturnal bloomers. These plants produce the largest and the most beau-

tiful flowers of all the cacti. Their blooms begin to open at sunset and, emitting a delightful vanilla-like aroma, reach full development during the night; then wither and die at dawn. Perhaps the most gorgeous flowers borne by any night-blooming cactus are those of *Selenicereus grandiflorus,* one of the species named "queen of the night." The globular, cup-shaped blossoms are a foot long and eight inches wide, white on the inside, yellow on the outside.

FRUITS

It is no simple task to describe completely the fruits of the cacti. There is a tremendous variation in the color, shape, and taste among the different species. In most cases the fruit is fleshy and berry like, ranging from an inch to about three inches in size. None of the Cactaceae bear poisonous fruit. But while many species have edible fruits, not all of these are of the same quality.

A collection of cactus fruits is as multicolored as an artist's pallette. They come in various shades of green, purple, red, and violet, as well as glossy pink, lilac, yellow, and white. The pulp—which may be sweet, slightly acid, or in some instances have the flavor of strawberries or pineapple—is also attractively hued.

The outer skin differs from species to species, being thick in some instances, thin in others. Similarly, fruit may be soft or hard, juicy or dry. Although, as indicated, the fruit is usually berry like, not all of it is round. Some are elliptical, elongated, globular, oval, pear or spindle shaped.

While some fruit is smooth, others are covered with scales, woolly or silk-like hairs, bristles—which may fall off when the fruit matures—and varying numbers of spines. The fruit of certain cacti have areoles. Frequently, other fruit or flowers sprout from these areoles. In fact, even the unripened fruit of

An Opuntia vulgaris varie-gata—*its pads are vividly marked with contrasting green, white and pink, earning the common name* Joseph's coat.

"Irish mittens" (*Opuntia monacantha*) will root and grow. Incidentally, *monacantha*, a native of South America, gets its common name from the appearance of its flattened, almost spineless, bright green joints.

A year may pass before the fruit of some of the Cactaceae matures. The more delicious of the edible varieties are prized by both man and birds. However, the latter dine on all types of cactus fruit and, unlike man, pay for their feasts. They disperse the seed which are scattered through the pulp like the seeds of a watermelon.

Some fruits contain only one relatively large seed. Others envelop a great many small ones. Generally, the seeds are a dull

33

Prickly pear laden with fruit. Note the spines on the plant's fleshy pads.

brown or glossy black but vary in form, being angular, flat, oval, boat, cup, or kidney shaped. They also may be minutely pitted, warty, winged, or covered with tiny tubercules.

2. "Nature ... makes all things serve their purpose."

Man has mixed feelings about cacti. Some gardeners think them the ugliest of plants. Others find beauty in their weird growth and exotic shapes. Certain Indians of the American Southwest hold various Cactaceae sacred, but ranchers in the same region consider them a nuisance. Similarly, in countries were a number of cacti have been introduced, the plants are either highly regarded or their importation is regretted.

None of the Cactaceae have been so highly prized in one locality and so heartily despised in another as those species of *Opuntia* that support the webs of the cochineal insect (*Coccus cacti*). Until chemists successfully compounded red dyes from coal tar, cochineal insects were used to color a wide variety of items ranging from cloth to candy. The raising of these tiny creatures is still carried on in countries as far apart as India and Mexico. This is because modern technology has been unable to produce a rich crimson hue called carmine from coal tar. Carmine is employed in making artist's colors and in the manufacture of beverages, cosmetics, and food. However, its most valuable use is in the laboratory where it serves as a stain to bring out the structure of animal cells and tissue.

Long before any European ventured across the Atlantic, the Aztecs were brushing cochineal insects off the stems of *Nopalea cochenillifera*, a more or less spineless, treelike cactus, and catching them in bags. The insects were then killed by heat,

Dense prickly pear, Opuntia inermis, *growing in Casuarina scrub pines, in Queensland, Australia, in 1926.*

The same area, three years later. The prickly pear have been destroyed by Cactoblastis cactorum—*biological control. Cochineal insects can be seen on two regrowth segments in left foreground.*

dried, and pulverized—some seventy thousand of them making a pound of dye. The Aztec word for this dye was *nocheztli* (blood of the nopal cactus).

Nocheztli was so valuable in ancient Mexico that Montezuma demanded sacks of cochineal as tribute from conquered peoples. The Spanish invaders were quick to see the commercial possibilities of the dye and began shipping cochineal home as early as 1523. But it was not until the middle of the seventeenth century that Cornelius Van Drebbel, a Dutch chemist, devised a method of dying wool a permanent red with cochineal.

Van Drebbel's discovery was of particular value to the British Army, whose uniform jackets were the source of the nickname "redcoats." Therefore, it is not surprising that Admiral Arthur Phillip (1737–1814), the first governor of New South Wales, Australia, imported opuntias and cochineal insects from Brazil "in order to dye his soldiers' coats red."

While Sir Arthur had good intentions, he unknowingly upset the balance of nature. Unhampered by natural enemies in their new home, the imported prickly pears spread rapidly, thanks to seed-carrying birds. By the early 1920's, some sixty million acres of farms and ranchlands were covered with cacti. In areas where the soil was rich, their formidable spines formed an impenetrable barrier five feet tall.

The Commonwealth Prickly Pear Board organized by the Australian government was ordered to destroy as many of the cacti as possible and to devise some method of stopping the advance of the plants into new areas. It tried chemicals, fire, and plowing without success. In desperation, the Board then imported approximately 150 kinds of plant-eating insects from the New World. Unfortunately, most of these immigrants found the crops of Australian farmers far more appealing than the prickly pears. But *Cactoblastis cactorum*, a moth from Argentina, was content with feeding on opuntias. Its caterpillar burrowed into the stems of the cacti, ate their sappy tissue, and so weakened the plants that they died.

In time, *Cactoblastis* reclaimed vast stretches of farm and grazing lands—the most outstanding example of the biological control of a weed. Today, the prickly pear is no longer a threat to the Australian economy. Yet, strangely enough, *Cactoblastis* does not normally feed on the species of opuntias imported by Admiral Phillip. There is good reason. None of them are native to Argentina!

Friend and Foe

American ranchers have no use for cacti. However, when grazing is poor and hay in short supply, they have been forced to use the spineless "Indian fig" (*Opuntia ficus-indica*) for fodder or to burn the spines off other opuntias and use their stems for feed. But starving cattle have never waited for their owners to prepare these emergency rations. Driven by hunger, they browse on cactus joints. As a result, their mouths and faces bristle with spines which often cause infections. Moreover, grazing cattle frequently brush against cacti. This may detach joints which become imbedded in their hides. While these "hitchhikers" usually fall off before causing any damage, they are apt to root wherever they strike the ground. Thus, unwittingly, the cattle spread plants that lessen the value of grazing land.

Although it is common for pack rats to carry the multi-barbed joints of various cholla considerable distances in order to protect the entrances to their dens and for cactus wrens to build their tunnel-like nests on the top of a cholla, cowboys cannot understand how these little creatures avoid the spines. No experienced puncher in the Southwest will mount a horse unless he is wearing *chaparajos* (wide leather pants open at the

Deep within the spines of this teddy-bear cholla, a cactus wren has built its covered nest which resembles "a desert version of an igloo." The tunnel entrance shows clearly.

back). Even the slight breeze created by a passing horse can break off a spine-studded cholla joint. "Chaps" prevent torn trousers and lacerated legs.

But despite the cowboys' dislike for cacti, the plants play an important part in the tall tales they tell "dudes." One of these yarns is an old Mexican folk tale that recounts what happened to a man who was carrying a proclamation to "a village whose name is no longer remembered." When the messenger stopped at an adobe hut to water his horse at dusk, he was urged to rest until morning as his route took him through the haunted desert where spirits roamed at night. Laughing at the warning, the messenger rode away and entered the desert.

For hours all went well. Then, suddenly, the horse stopped and the messenger was mysteriously grabbed and held in a vise-like grip. The more he struggled, the tighter he was held. Convinced that he had been seized by spirits, the helpless rider sat motionless in the saddle until dawn. Then he discovered he was caught in a cholla!

Strangely enough, although the men who ride the range in the Southwest are fond of telling stories about cacti, they have no patience with the Mexicans and Indians who claim cholla joints actually jump at anyone who passes. Nevertheless, cattlemen always refer to a cholla as a "jumping cactus."

Moreover, whenever punchers pass a cholla they invariably look for a cactus cat. This fantastic "critter" can be easily identified. Its hairs resemble cactus spines—the hairs on the ears are very still and long—while the tail branches like cholla joints. But the most remarkable feature of the cactus cat is its hairless forelegs. They are shaped like the blade of a butcher's knife and are razor sharp. Cowboys, who, as everyone knows, *never* lie when telling a tale, swear that the cactus cat uses its forelegs to slash cholla in order to tap sap. Swinging in a loop "as wide as a herd of Texas steers," the cactus cat slashes a great number of cacti.

By the time the cat completes this circuit the sap in the first cholla has fermented, making a sweet, intoxicating drink. Lapping up the sap, the animal goes from plant to plant until it "becomes fiddling drunk and goes waltzing off in the moonlight grasping its bony forelegs across each other and screaming with delight."

As is to be expected, none of the zoologists—students of animal life—who have investigated the habits of the wildlife of the Southwest have ever seen a cactus cat. Indeed, they never will —the cactus cat exists only in the imagination of the cowboy. However, zoologists have discovered there is a close interdependence between birds and cacti. The former depend upon the plants for food and nesting sites—it is estimated that half the bird population of the American desert would perish were it not for the Cactaceae—while the latter rely on the birds to spread their seeds.

Incidentally, the cacti that grow on the slopes that border Death Valley, an extremely arid desert in eastern California which contains the lowest point of dry land in the United States, provide fodder for about a thousand burros. These descendants of the patient beasts that once served miners as pack animals are true relics of the Old West. Nevertheless, their future is doubtful. Some conservationists would destroy them, arguing that burros are not native inhabitants of the region and their grazing on the sparse desert vegetation is ecologically unsound. Other individuals claim that the burros should be preserved because of their history. However, the burros' defenders think their numbers should be limited so that nature's balance will not be upset. Meanwhile, the burros pay no more attention

A clump of organ pipe cactus framed against a background of rugged mountains in southwestern Arizona.

to man than they do to the spines on a juice-filled prickly-pear pad.

STRANGE PARTNERS

Thousands of miles from the cholla thickets of the Americas, a reptile has a close association with various species of *Opuntia*. The reptile is one of the most fascinating of all creatures, the giant tortoise, *Testudo elephantopus*. It inhabits the Galapagos Archipelago, a group of volcanic islands straddling the Equator some six hundred miles west of Ecuador.

Scientists theorize that opuntias carried by ocean currents reached the Galapagos before the tortoises. At any rate, cacti are the only green vegetation on the islands during the long dry season. By feeding on prickly-pear joints and fruit during this period, the tortoises have survived.

Over the years, tortoises on the more arid islands have developed saddle-shaped shells and long necks, a combination that enables them to reach up and graze. Meanwhile, the opuntias developed a defense against the hungry reptiles. By degrees their tender seedlings became completely covered with spines.

LEFT TO RIGHT: *Three beautiful cacti*—Trichocereus bridgesii, *with deep ribs and yellow-orange spines;* Gymnocalycium denudatum, *one of the chin cacti so called because of the chins under each areole;* Mammillaria tegelbergiana, *named for a famous nurseryman.*

Then, as the plants matured, the lower spines disappeared, being replaced by an unpalatable woody bark. However, the full-grown opuntias continued to satisfy the hungry reptiles. As their pads filled out during the rainy season they became heavy and dropped. Today, as for many years, the fallen pads and fruit remain succulent on the ground and provide the tortoises with food during the annual drought. Meanwhile, the reptiles' feces fertilize next year's crop of seedlings.

On islands where no tortoises have ever lived the opuntias are low shrubs. But where the giant reptiles are found, the cacti have become treelike, some varieties attaining a trunk diameter of more than four feet. On these islands, tortoises have very long necks. Thus the plants and the reptiles have evolved into their present forms in direct relation to one another.

LEGEND AND FACT

When the Earth was young—so the story goes—the rain-god and the wind-god were close friends who enjoyed playing practical jokes on one another. One day as the rain-god was watering the fields and forests his chum blew so hard that all the drops dried up before reaching the ground.

For some reason this prank made the rain-god angry. He withdrew to his magic castle, swearing never to send water earthward again. As a result, animals and plants died of thirst and the sun-baked soil became as hard as an arrowhead.

Worried about the drought and sincerely sorry he had offended his old friend, the wind-god sent his daughter to the magic castle with an apology and a plea for rain. For days the maiden, suffering from heat and exhaustion, walked toward the castle. Finally, she fell and managed to crawl into the shade of a prickly pear where she went to sleep. When she awoke the next morning she saw some berries on the cactus, rubbed off their spines, and ate them. Refreshed by her sleep and the

This ancient Peruvian ceramic vessel is decorated with painted cacti—they appear to be prickly pears.

juicy fruit, she continued her journey.

She was now in the desert but there was no danger of her wandering in circles as so many people do when they lose all sense of direction. Rows of *Opuntia* forced the maid to walk in a narrow path. From time to time the wind-god's daughter rested in the shade of the cacti and satisfied her hunger with their fruit. Eventually, the path led her to the mysterious castle.

The cloud guards ushered her to their master. At first, the rain-god refused to accept his friend's apology or agree to send water to the parched Earth. But the girl was both beautiful and persuasive and he finally relented. When the two gods were reunited they decided that *Opuntia* should be rewarded for saving the maiden's life and guiding her. Therefore they decreed that a section of land should be set aside for the prickly pear where it would rain just enough to keep the plants healthy but not enough to cause them to rot. From that time to this—as everyone knows—it rarely rains in the desert.

Like the wind-god's daughter, the prospectors of yesteryear

who trekked across the American desert seeking a legendary mine were grateful to cacti. The fruit of the prickly pear made their diet of sourdough biscuits and strong coffee more appetizing. Many a "desert rat" managed to survive under the blazing sun when his canteen was empty and the water holes were dry by drinking cactus juice.

The plants that quenched their thirst are popularly known as barrel cacti. This is a most appropriate name. Not only are these desert drinking fountains shaped like a barrel but also they contain large amounts of water. Months after a rain their white pulp is full of moisture. To get at this liquid the top of the plant is cut off, the pulp crushed and squeezed, and the juice caught as it oozes through the mass.

There are many documented records of persons lost in the desert drinking cactus juice. Among these are statements of Air Force pilots who parachuted into the desert and wandered about until rescued. Although certain authorities claim that it is impossible for anyone weakened from exhaustion to topple a tall barrel cactus, actually, it is quite easy because the plants have extremely shallow roots. Even a South American species

Even relatively small barrel cacti are expensive. Those shown here sell from fifty to sixty-five dollars each.

that grows ten feet tall and is three or four feet in diameter—such a specimen may weigh ten tons—can be felled with a vigorous kick. Its roots barely reach below the surface. Obviously, such a root system offers but slight support to such heavy plants. Indeed, barrel cacti frequently tumble from their own weight after sopping up water in periods of exceptionally heavy rains. But being prostrate makes no difference—the plant thrives because the roots continue to supply it with water.

Besides providing water in emergencies, barrel cacti can be used as a compass. Influenced by the rays of the mid-day sun, they usually lean toward the south. However, a lost individual should bear in mind that this is a general rule. He should never rely on one or two plants to determine direction but check a number of plants to orient himself.

Cacti as Food

The most delicious fruits borne by the Cactaceae are those of various opuntias. Like the flattened, jointed stems of the plants on which they develop, these fruits are pear shaped—a double reason for the popular name "prickly pear." It is not easy to avoid the cushions of fine barbed bristles when peeling the fruit, but both Indian and Mexican women perform the task with as much ease as they pluck the berries from the almost spineless *Opuntia ficus-indica*.

However, if Apache lore is true, all cacti with edible fruit were once densely covered with needle-like spines. As a result, the early redmen had great difficulty in harvesting the fruit. But Killer of Enemies, a legendary demi-god who watched over the Apaches, took pity on his people. Using his knowledge of magic, Killer of Enemies caused most of the spines to vanish.

Killer of Enemies must have been a very powerful magician.

OPPOSITE: Gigante *cactus—the black spots are seeds.*

46

How else can one explain the lack of spines on *Opuntia ficus-indica*? Actually, because the nourishing and refreshing fruit of this cactus is easily picked, it is a staple food of Indians in both North and South America. In fact, the widespread use of its fruit is the source of the plant's common name of Indian fig. But the Indians are not the only ones to prize prickly pears. They are relished in many subtropical countries where opuntias are indigenous or have been introduced.

The Indian fig is not the only opuntia to be imported by man into warm countries. A number of species with edible fruits—differing in size, sweetness, color, and size of seeds—have been shipped to other lands. But of them all, the common prickly pear is considered the most valuable. This is because it furnishes food to humans and can be used to fatten livestock and pigs. Moreover, the practically spineless stems supply green fodder during subtropical summers when grass frequently dries up because of the excessive heat.

Besides offering prickly pears to their customers, the fruit vendors of Mexico stock several other varieties of cactus fruit. The round red berries of *Opuntia streptacantha*—popularly known as "tuna cardona"—sell well. Mexicans use the sweet

Of all cacti, the opuntias are the most valuable economically. Note the varying forms of the pads on these specimens.

pulp of this fruit to make preserves and an alcoholic drink. *Garambullos*, the small, blue, olive-shaped berries of *Myrtillocactus geometrizans*, are also a favorite of Mexicans.

Generally speaking, all cactus fruit has a pleasant taste. However, the berries of certain species have a distinct musky flavor. But they are counterbalanced by *Echinocereus stramineus*. Its crisp, juicy, brownish-red fruit tastes like strawberries. While the Indians considered the fruit of the "strawberry cactus" particularly delicious, cactus collectors prize the plant because of its sensitivity to light. As soon as the sun sets, a strawberry cactus closes its funnel-shaped blooms and "goes to sleep."

While all Indian tribes in the Southwest, as well as in Central and South America, ate cactus fruit when it was available— and still do—the berries were most important to the Pimas and Papagos of Arizona. Not only did they consider the fruits a delicacy but also they ground the stems of prickly pears to extract their rich sugar content.

Today, enterprising businessmen seeking to profit from the hordes of tourists who visit the Southwest annually have borrowed the practice from the Indians and manufacture cactus candy. This is made by boiling down the pulp of the barrel cactus, passing the liquid through strainers, and then hardening it. Packaged in boxes decorated with desert scenes, the candy makes a most attractive and tasty souvenir.

But the Indians of the Southwest consider the reddish-purple fruits, which resemble tiny cucumbers, of the saguaro far more delectable than cactus candy. Therefore, when the berries mature in late June, the Pima and Papago set up harvest camps near saguaro stands and gather tons of the fruit. While much of it is eaten fresh, large amounts are preserved in their own sugar for later use or made into jam. Juice extracted from the fruit is boiled down to a molasses-like syrup which is stored in pottery jars—a supply of sweeting that lasts until the next harvest. The mass of tiny black seeds that are strained from the pulp are ground into meal and pressed into cakes.

Saguaro fruit is so important to the Papagos that they celebrate its harvesting with a festival. Before the white man imposed his calendar upon the Indians this event marked the start of the Papago New Year.

Botanists have discovered that a saguaro will bear fruit annually for as long as three years without receiving a drop of rain. But long before scientists studied the life cycle of the giant cactus, the Indians knew they could rely upon it to furnish them with food. Proof of this is the meaning of "saguaro." It is a Spanish word derived from the Pima word for friend.

CACTUS "LUMBER"

Few foreigners spend the night at the hotel in Cachi, a small town in northern Argentina. Those that do are astounded to discover that the hotel's beams, floors, and doorsills are made of cacti. Actually, this is not a unique situation in the semiarid regions of Central and South America where lumber is scarce.

Many Mexicans live in cactus-framed houses plastered with adobe. Moreover, throughout Central America, native craftsmen fashion furniture from the woody skeletons of the saguaro. In the same area carpenters make window frames from cactus stems.

The long, slender, tapering, tough, woody ribs which form a tube inside saguaro tissue and support the plants in high winds are excellent substitutes for lumber. Ranchers use these ribs to build shelters and corrals, while novelty manufacturers make planters and other small items from saguaro "wood" for the tourist trade.

The Papago employ the ribs of the giant cactus for many different purposes, including roofing their houses and making cradles. However, both white and red men may have to turn to

50

The ribs of the giant saguaro are used by the Indians for building. Note the holes made by the woodpeckers for nests.

some other building material.

Some years ago, the National Park Service which has supervision over the finest stands of saguaros in the United States noted that a bacteria-caused rot was killing off the plants. A campaign was immediately launched to save the giant cacti. Among the methods employed to check the disease was injecting them with penicillin, one of the earliest uses of that wonder drug. While the future of the saguaros is still in doubt, hopefully, the bacterium that destroys them—it is carried in the intestine of a tiny night-flying moth whose larvae live in saguaro tissue—will be eliminated. Otherwise, *Cereus giganteus*, which has come to be the symbol of the American Southwest, will disappear.

Not only would this be an aesthetic loss but also it would cause irreparable damage to the wildlife that depends upon the saguaro for food and shelter. For example, it is believed that the elf owl will only brood in the holes made by woodpeckers in saguaros. The woodpeckers use these cavities for a year as a nest and then chisel out another while the owls sublet their old apartments. Incidentally, the excavations made by the woodpeckers do not harm the cacti if they are made during the dry season. The plants line them with a callous-like growth.

Paradoxically, even as man strives to save the giant cacti from extinction from rot, he well may be responsible for their total destruction in the United States. Not only has the farmer's plow turned over thousands of acres of saguaro-dotted land but also the hoofs of cattle have trampled to death countless saguaro seedlings. Moreover, hunters and trappers have killed vast numbers of coyotes, eagles, and hawks in the mistaken belief that they destroy great numbers of domestic fowl, small game, calves, and lambs every year. By so doing, they have made it possible for the desert's rodent population—the normal prey of the slain predators—to increase tremendously.

52

Since many of these rodents are seed-eaters—some actually scamper up the spiny stems of saguaros to get at their fruit—and the giant cacti reproduce only by seeds, man has upset the balance of nature. Yet, at first thought, it would appear that the seed-eaters pose no threat to the saguaro since each plant produces several million seeds during its lifetime. However, it is possible that every one of these seeds will be eaten by a rodent.

Sacred and Holy

Oasis-dwellers in the Syrian Desert surround their property with high mud fences topped with prickly pears to keep out stray animals. Farmers in Central America enclose fields with cacti to protect them. The natives of Curaçao, an island off the coast of Venezuela, hang their washing on cacti and use the spines for clothespins.

But the Indians of the Southwest and Mexico would never employ cacti for such purposes. To these tribesmen the plants are sacred. The Zuni classify the cactus as one of the plants that "give of themselves to the people." So highly do the Zuni hold cacti that bear edible fruit that when a member of the Zuni Cactus Society—a group charged with the control of game and the curing of wounds—approaches the cactus to be used in the ritual whipping of a chief, he carries a specially beaded prayer feather.

Other southwestern tribes also have cactus societies that conduct ceremonial whippings with cacti. These lashings supposedly make an individual strong and brave. The Hano also beat the ground with cactus stems, believing that this would cause the ground to freeze and thus their warriors would leave no tracks.

During their seasonal visits to the pueblo of Acoma, certain kachinas—masked representatives of ancient gods—carry cactus stems. Those men who manage to rub against the stems are

ABOVE LEFT: Ancistocactus scheeri, *the wait-a-bit cactus, has sharply recurved spines.* RIGHT: Thrixanthocereus blossfeldiorum *is a tall-growing species.* BELOW LEFT: Notocactus grassessneri *has soft yellow-orange spines.* CENTER: Notocactus braziliensis *has downward-pointing spines.* RIGHT: Mammillaria echinaria *is a columnar species.*

convinced that they will have more vigor. Meanwhile, the Hopi place bits of cactus in the corners of their houses "to give them roots."

Cacti are also employed in the secret rites held in the kivas —the enclosed chambers where the pueblo-dwellers conduct religious ceremonies. While few of these rituals have been observed by outsiders, some individuals have seen the "Cactus Grandmother" of the Tewa display its magical properties.

The "Cactus Grandmother" is actually a section of cactus stem. During the rite it is passed from hand to hand around a kiva three times. If it is dropped, all present are doomed to ill fortune. As the stem passes from person to person it gets smaller and smaller and finally vanishes. But when the leader of the ceremony goes to a certain place in the kiva he finds the "Cactus Grandmother" intact.

Many Indians hold that cacti make potent "lucky pieces." Mexican tribesmen often tuck a bit of cactus in their belts to insure success while hunting. The reason why the native peoples of Mexico associate cacti with magic can be traced to a very old folk tale dealing with the establishment of the first Aztec community.

No one knows for sure where the Aztecs originated, but tradition states that they migrated south from a cold land. Their chief deity, Mexitli, told their leaders to keep traveling until they came upon a great eagle perched on a cactus devouring a snake. After years of wandering, the headmen saw the omen that Mexitli had promised. The Aztecs built their homes at the spot where the cactus grew. Today, the community they founded is called Mexico City after Mexitli, and the omen that led to its establishment appears both on the seal and the flag of the Republic of Mexico.

Aduana was once a thriving Mexican mining town. Today, it is almost deserted. Only a few buildings have withstood years of

Cacti appear on the seal of Mexico.

neglect and the effects of the weather, but the Church of Santa Baluanera has suffered little damage. Moreover, the cactus that grows out of one of the church's thick walls is as healthy as it was some 150 years ago.

Legend holds that Santa Baluanera stands on the site of an enclosure built around the cactus by a band of Indians who became Christians after seeing a vision of the Virgin Mary. This apparition appeared to them sitting on the top of a giant cactus with arms held out as if asking to be rescued. To reach the Virgin the Indians began erecting a ramp of stones. As they rolled the stones into place, a rich vein of silver was unearthed and the vision vanished.

Convinced that the stories of the Virgin's kindness told to them by missionaries were true, the Indians not only agreed to conversion but also constructed the shrine that eventually became Aduana's church.

Residents of the surrounding countryside make an annual pilgrimage to Aduana to see the cactus and to pray. This is not the only instance where Cactaceae and Christianity are united. During Holy Week in a number of out-of-the-way canyons in the United States and in isolated Mexican villages, a once common but now rare rite is celebrated—devout groups re-enact the passion of Christ and flagellate themselves with cactus stems.

Long before the coming of the white man, many Indian tribes were using *Lophopora williamsii*, a spineless, gray-green "button" cactus covered with white hairs, in religious ceremonies. Commonly called "peyote," this native of northern Mexico and Texas contains mescaline, a mild, non-addictive hallucinogen that produces imaginary perceptions of objects and events and affects sight and hearing.

The Indians chewed peyote or brewed it into tea in order to have visions, cure illness, bring luck, overcome enemies, increase endurance, or talk to their gods. They still do—and the battle as to whether or not peyote is the "divine intoxicant" of the Aztecs or the "diabolical root" of the Spanish priests continues to be waged.

No one knows when the Indians began using peyote as a hallucinogen. However, it has been established that the early residents of the Southwest and of Central America not only used the cactus as a medicine but also ritually ate dry or green peyote buttons in order to foretell the future, find lost objects, and combat witchcraft.

Because peyote grows only in a few small areas it is not easily found. This is the source of the legends that detail the ability of the plant to conceal itself or to "sink in the ground like a mole" if those who seek it have not purified themselves. Conversely, other legends hold that peyote sings so that man can locate it. These tales also state that peyote is a woman and those who are fortunate can hear her singing at rituals honoring the plant.

No primitive Indians consider peyote more sacred than the Huichol of Mexico. They claim the cactus was once a deer. Therefore, the music for their peyote dances is furnished by deer-hoof rattles and notched deer bones rubbed together. The

This round, spineless, and unattractive specimen is actually a cluster of one of the most fascinating of cacti. These five "buttons" are peyote, a cactus that has influenced Indian culture for centuries.

Huichol also dramatize the traditional kinship between peyote and the deer in the rites they perform before setting out on a hunt.

Peyote does not grow in the area inhabited by the Huichol, who employ the plant as a medicine for a long list of ills as well as for fortune-telling, amulets, and religious purposes. Therefore, these Indians travel northward to the state of San Luis Potosi to gather the cactus—a journey that traditionally takes forty-three days. Those who make the trip engage in elaborate purifying ceremonies before starting out and at intervals along the way.

As they trek northward, the Huichol sing of Jiculi, a cultural hero who was captured by witches, confined in a cage, but escaped with the aid of the animals and birds. However, the witches followed Jiculi's tracks and were about to overtake him when the gods changed him into a deer so that he could run more swiftly. But the witches transformed themselves into dogs and surrounded Jiculi. Just as they leaped at their victim, the gods again interfered. They changed the deer into the peyote plant, which helps the Huichol just as Jiculi did when he was alive.

Meanwhile, increasing numbers of Indians throughout the Americas have become convinced that God created peyote so that man could communicate directly with Him without the aid of a minister, priest, or rabbi. As a result, the Native American Church of the United States—which combines ancient peyote ceremonies with modern religious thought—has been organized. Although the use of peyote is forbidden by law in several states, there is no federal mandate against it.

3. "...take pleasure with the beauty of growing plants."

To the learned men who were members of the Spanish court in the early sixteenth century, the plants included in the cargoes of the galleons that bore the treasures of the New World to the Old were almost as valuable as gold and silver. None of these plants fascinated them more than the few specimens of Cactaceae collected by the priests who had accompanied the conquistadors. While certain of these cacti were successfully transplanted, most of them died.

As a matter of fact, there was no widespread cultivation of cacti in Europe until it became fashionable for wealthy men to grow exotic plants in greenhouses. Yet, while these individuals prided themselves on their cactus collections, they actually displayed very few species. It was not until the early nineteenth century that a large variety of cacti were shipped across the Atlantic. Meanwhile, the Cactaceae were not popular house or garden plants in America.

Today, countless gardeners in the United States—along with their counterparts throughout the civilized world—raise cacti. Few of these individuals own greenhouses or live in regions where cacti may be planted in beds. The majority of cactus growers are windowsill gardeners.

Actually, no plants adjust more readily to the hot, dry atmosphere of the average dwelling than cacti. Their demands are

This greenhouse bench shows a wide variety in shape and type of cacti.

This collection of mature cacti has been displayed in many flower shows. One of the most unusual in the group is the magnificent crested plant behind the pole on the right.

few—light, careful watering, and a well-drained growing medium.

LIGHT

Most cacti are light-demanding. Therefore, Cactaceae should
never be placed far from a window unless artificial light is pro-
vided. The latter is best furnished by any of the fluorescent
light tubes especially designed for indoor gardening. While fix-
tures for these tubes are relatively inexpensive—their price depends upon their length—many young cactus collectors make
their own from sheet metal under the guidance of a "shop"
instructor at school or a parent at home. Another way to ac-
quire a fluorescent unit cheaply is to get one from an electri-
cian who has replaced an old but working fixture with a more
modern one. Furthermore, rather than give individual presents
at Christmas or on birthdays, friends and relatives are usually
delighted to make a joint purchase of a fluorescent setup as a
gift.

Whether used in a standard or home-made fixture—which
should be hung horizontally—the tubes should be placed six to
ten inches above the cacti, depending upon the size of the
plants. The best results are achieved by the combination of a
"daylight" tube and a "natural" tube. The former emits violet
and blue rays, the latter orange and red. Plants need both types
of rays to grow well. Since cacti should have approximately
fourteen hours of light daily when fluorescent tubes are used, it
is convenient—but by no means necessary—to attach a timer to
the unit which will turn the tubes on and off automatically.
Incidentally, a timer can be adjusted so that the tubes not only
provide "sunshine" but also serve as a night light. This pre-
vents stumbling over furniture in the dark and also acts as a
determent to burglars.

Under fluorescent tubes, all parts of a plant receive an equal amount of light. However, if one side of a cactus is constantly exposed to the direct rays of the sun, it may "burn." Therefore, Cactaceae grown in bright sunny windows should be turned weekly. Species that require indirect light will thrive on the "dark" side of a dwelling or if placed between taller plants where they are partially shaded.

Incidentally, it is a common practice for commercial cactus growers to attach tags to their products which not only give the popular and Latin names of a plant but also its place of origin, growth habits, and water and light requirements. Here is a typical tag:

TROPICAL QUEEN OF THE NIGHT
(*Hylocereus undatus*)

✿

Native of Brazil
This is a fast-growing cactus that
will develop into a large plant. The
white flowers are nocturnal (bloom
at night). Keep in partial shade
moderately moist.

WATERING

More cacti are killed by overwatering than in any other way. Yet it is not easy to answer the questions when to water, how often, and how much? The difficulty is that Cactaceae must be kept between two extremes—shriveling from lack of water or rotting from too much.

Generally speaking, most cacti require very little water during the winter when they are dormant. However, plants kept on a sunny windowsill near a radiator may demand considerable moisture. The best procedure is to water, allow the soil to dry out at least to a depth of an inch, then water again. But at the

Easily raised in pot, hanging basket, or grafted on sturdy understock to form a pyramid, the Easter cactus repays the care it receives with a profusion of blooms.

same time it must be remembered that certain species require water only once in three weeks. Then, too, winter bloomers such as the so-called Christmas and other crab cacti should be watered as long as they are in flower.

The safest rule is to underwater in winter since, as indicated, cacti are capable of withstanding long droughts. However, as days grow brighter and growth starts, more water is needed. Some experts advocate frequent light waterings during the summer. Others prefer a thorough soaking once a month.

Obviously, there is no hard and fast rule for watering cacti. Nevertheless, beginners will lose few plants if they water them just enough to prevent their drying completely in winter and keep them moist, not wet, in the summer.

In cities where chlorine is employed to purify the water supply, special care must be taken. Tap water in these localities should be "aged" before use. This is easily done by storing it in an unstoppered gallon jug. As a matter of fact, it is good prac-

64

tice to age chlorine-free water as well, to insure that it will be at room temperature—cacti dislike cold baths! The best time to water is in the morning before the plants are flooded with sunshine. This is because water on the stem and branches may act like a lens and concentrate the sun's rays so that the plant is burned. Moreover, when the temperature is high, evaporation is rapid and the plant doesn't benefit from all the water applied.

POTTING

Cacti do not require rich soil. But their growing medium must be porous and permeable. With the exception of the few species that have special requirements, the packaged "cactus potting soil" sold in garden shops is suitable for most Cactaceae. However, if large amounts of this mix are needed, it is quite expensive. Therefore, it is far cheaper to compound the following:

2 parts sharp sand
2 parts loam
1 part old brick pounded into bits
½ part peat moss

Flat of golden ball cacti ready for transplanting

Flat of Cereus Peruvianus *ready for transplanting*

Rural residents can substitute leaf mold (half-rotten leaves) for peat moss, damaged clay pots for bricks, and collect the other ingredients at practically no cost. City dwellers probably will have to buy both loam and peat moss—which can be purchased in small amounts. A polite request to the foreman of the wrecking crew demolishing an old building will usually result in the gift of one or two bricks. Sand can be gathered from a beach. But sand taken from the seaside must be soaked in a bucket of frequently changed fresh water to remove any salt content.

A kitchen table covered with newspapers is an ideal place to prepare potting soil. The best tool for mixing is one's hands. Before any soil is put into the pots, they should be at least one-third filled with "crock"—gravel or pieces of broken clay pots. If available, a few chunks of charcoal will help keep the mixture "sweet."

Cacti resent chemical fertilizers but a pinch of bone meal per pot is appreciated. Moreover, as most Cactaceae prefer a calaceous soil, it is well to add a small amount of lime or finely crushed clam or eggshells to each potful of the growing medium.

Transplanting cacti poses no problems if they are planted no deeper in their new pot—which should be just slightly larger than the previous container—than in the old one. Mature cacti should be placed in the center of a pot. Plant seedlings at one side, which will encourage their roots to spread. After transplanting Cactaceae of any size, keep them shaded for a week and spray the plants with water daily. Then move into light and water as necessary.

If possible, plunge potted cacti into the ground during the summer months. An outdoor vacation perks them up tremendously.

This cluster, while attractive, should be repotted. Pots should be half as tall as the height of a tall plant, one inch wider than a round plant.

LEFT: *Dark brown with harmless spines,* Copiapoa humilis *forms clusters when it reaches maturity.*

BELOW: *Although the opuntia pad in the foreground is not ready for potting, it has developed two new shoots. The cereus cutting on the left has shriveled while becoming calloused but will fill out when watered.*

PROPAGATION

The cheapest way to add to a cactus collection is to propagate new plants from cuttings, which are sections of a plant removed with a sharp, clean knife. Cuttings can also be made from off-shoots, the branches of the main stem that usually rise from the base of the "mother plant."

Either an entire joint or a small section of the stem can be used for a cutting. Whether large or small, cuttings should be placed in a dry, shaded spot until calluses form at their base. This takes from a week to more than a month, depending upon the size of the cut. The wider the cut, the longer the healing process.

To root callused cuttings, insert them in a pot filled with sand and powdered charcoal. Care should be taken that the cuttings are not too deeply planted. Top-heavy and tall cuttings will stand erect if tied to a support. Water cuttings sparingly or not at all until they form roots. Too much moisture will cause them to rot. If this occurs, cut back to healthy tissue and set the cutting aside to callus again.

As soon as roots form, a cutting may be permanently potted. Cuttings may also be rooted in the pots in which they are to remain. Prepare pots as directed, make a small depression in the growing medium, fill it with sand and powdered charcoal, and insert the cutting.

CACTI FROM SEED

Growing cacti from seed requires a great deal of patience. This is because, although most cactus seed is very fertile and germinates quickly, seedlings take a long time to develop into full-grown plants. Nevertheless, raising Cactaceae from seed is a fascinating activity.

It is not difficult to purchase seeds of common species. A package of one hundred seeds costs about fify cents. Seeds of rare varieties are far more expensive and can only be procured from specialists who advertise in garden magazines. However, most rare cacti are grown from seeds. This is because of Federal regulations that control the importation of plants, as well as state laws designed to protect endangered species.

Cactus seeds may be grown in any container that is well drained. Before using, sterilize by flooding with boiling water. The gravel placed in the lower portion of the container and the growing mixture—equal parts of peat, loam, and coarse sand— should also be sterilized. This is best done by baking in an oven set at 150 degrees for approximately ten minutes.

Before planting the seeds, wet the mixture thoroughly, and let stand overnight. Cactus seeds should be scattered on the surface of the soil and merely pressed down gently with a flat object. Germination is best when the seeds are subjected to a temperature of 70 to 90 degrees. The soil should never be allowed to dry out but must be kept moist, not wet. Setting a pane of glass over the seed bed or enclosing it in a plastic bag will help retain the necessary moisture. As soon as the sprouts appear, they must be uncovered.

Although, as indicated, most cactus seeds germinate quickly, there is a variation in the time it takes the seeds of various species to sprout. When a package of "mixed seeds" is planted, some crack open in a very short time while others show no signs of life. But if the seed bed is given a heavy watering about a week after planting, usually a new crop of tiny cacti will appear.

GRAFTING

Grafting is the insertion of part of one plant (the cion) into a stem, root, or branch of another plant (the stock) so that a permanent union is effected. Through grafts, nurserymen have created apple trees that bear six or seven different types of

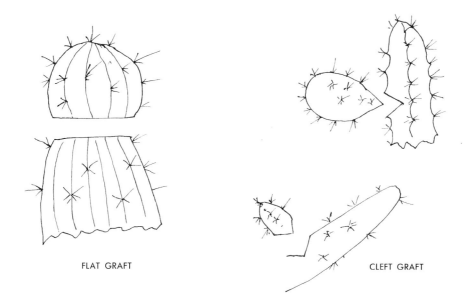

FLAT GRAFT

CLEFT GRAFT

apples and citrus trees that produce not only oranges but also lemons, grapefruit, and tangerines. But it is impossible to graft an apple cion onto a citrus tree.

However, unlike the majority of most plants, totally unrelated genera of Cactaceae can be grafted. As a result, drooping species can be joined to sturdy stock for the sake of appearance, rare specimens can be saved from rot, or the rate of growth increased by uniting a slow-growing species with one of relatively rapid growth. Along with these practical reasons for grafting cacti, growers combine different species for the fun of forming outlandishly shaped plants.

It is a rather complicated process to graft fruit trees and ornamental bushes. But no great skill nor special tools are needed to graft cacti during their growing season. Moreover, cactus tissue heals more quickly when grafted than does the tissue of other plants. As a result, most of these unions "take."

The easiest graft for a novice to attempt is the joining of a

71

The three cacti in the rear of this dish garden are mutations grafted on Triangularis. The grafts are various colors, making these "cactus bunnies" most attractive.

small globular species to a column-like cactus of similar diameter. With a sharp knife slice both the stock—which should be well-rooted and dry—and the cion so that the cuts form flat surfaces. Stock and cion must be joined together immediately. While experts often use long cactus spines to hold a graft in place, amateurs will find it best to bind their grafts with raffia. This is removed once cion and stock are bonded, and the grafted plant should thrive.

72

Examples of top grafting. The best time to join cion and understock is during the spring or summer when both are growing actively.

Grafting enables the cactus collector to force weak plants into strong growth and also to create curosities like those shown here.

These saguaro have been thoughtlessly vandalized by visitors to the Saguaro National Monument.

Except for the shape of the cuts, the same procedure is followed when grafts are made along the stem of the stock rather than its top. The cions are cut into a wedgelike shape and inserted into similar cuts in the stock.

"Sundry shapes or formes"

All cactus collectors have the same difficulty—they never have enough space for all the species they would like to grow. Therefore, beginners will do well to decide whether they want free-blooming cacti, species with multicolored spines, or oddities.

Of course, no matter what choice is made, some people will see no beauty in any cactus collection. But on closer inspection they may change their minds. For example, when railroad tycoon Henry E. Huntington was a young man, he backed into a cactus while working on the roadbed of the Southern Pacific. Years later, when Huntington built the famous combination library and art museum that bears his name in San Marino, California, and his gardener suggested landscaping the structure with cacti, Huntington—who prided himself on his memory—refused. However, he relented and eventually became so interested in the project that he brought trainloads of cacti and desert sand to San Marino and created one of the finest cactus gardens in the United States.

The more experience one has in raising cacti, the more in-

Areas such as this young and vigorous saguaro stand may well be the cactus forests of the future.

teresting they become. In fact, some people who have collected and cared for the plants for years are just as amazed at the structure of a newly acquired species as was the author of *The Herball or Generall Historie of Plantes* when he saw a turk's cap cactus for the first time in the late sixteenth century:

Who can but maruell at the rare and singular Workmanship which the Lord God almightie hath shewed in this thistle. . . . This knobbie or bunchie masse or lumpe is strangely compact and context togither, containing in it sundry shapes or formes.

Index

SIGMUND A. LAVINE was highly active while in college; he wrote features for the *Boston Sunday Post* and covered Boston University sports for two wire services. After receiving his M.A., he taught in a United States Government Indian School at Belcourt, North Dakota, for two years, learned to speak both the Sioux and Cree languages and talk in sign language. He was invited to tribal dances, ceremonies, and Indian Court in reservations throughout Canada and the Northwest.

Sigmund Lavine has taught in the Boston schools for over thirty years and is now an assistant principal. He also lectures and writes literary criticism.

With his wife—and a whippet answering to the unlikely name of Morrisey, the latest in a long line of prize-winning dogs owned by the Lavines—he lives in a house filled with books, fish tanks, historical china, art glass, and the largest privately owned collection of Gilbert and Sullivan material in America. For relaxation the Lavines attend country auctions, go "antiquing," or browse in bookstores, but their greatest pleasure is truck gardening on a piece of rocky New Hampshire land.

DATE DUE
